REACHING OUT

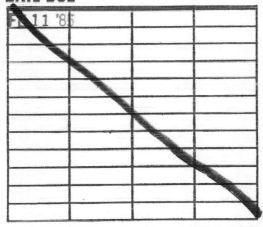

Perspectives on Gifted and Talented Education

REACHING OUT
Advocacy for the Gifted and Talented
American Association for Gifted Children

Perspectives on Gifted and Talented Education

Abraham J. Tannenbaum
Director

Elizabeth Neuman
Editor

Gifted and Talented Project
Teachers College, Columbia University

Teachers College, Columbia University
New York and London   1980

This work was developed under a contract with the U.S. Office of
Education, Department of Health, Education, and Welfare. However, the
content does not necessarily reflect the position or policy of that Agency,
and no official endorsement of these materials should be inferred.

Library of Congress Cataloging in Publication Data

American Association for Gifted Children.
   Reaching out.

   (Perspectives on gifted and talented education)
   Bibliography: p.
   Includes index.
   1. Gifted children—Education.   I. Title.
II. Series.
LC3993.A45 1980   371.95   80-14342
ISBN 0-8077-2591-9

Design by Romeo Enriquez

8   7   6   5   4   3   2   1   80   81   82   83   84   85   86   87

Printed in the U.S.A.

CONTENTS

FOREWORD

GIFTED CHILDREN WHO draw attention to themselves—and not all do—through their precocity are constantly in the public eye, sometimes as stars, sometimes as sties. They cannot be ignored, but they can be neglected. Professionals and laymen alike have often reacted ambivalently to these children, appreciating their special qualities while doubting their right to special educational enrichment on the grounds that it smacks of elitism. There are educators who believe that the gifted can make it on their own without extra help and regard differentiated programs for such children as luxuries that are welcome when they are affordable and quickly disposable when they are not. What counts most according to this point of view is the "golden mean," or normalcy, as reflected in the normal curve of ability and performance. Whoever fails to measure up to the golden mean has a right to every kind of compensatory assistance; whoever exceeds levels of functioning that are normal or average for most children may receive applause but no extra attention. Rarely is thought given to the possibility that democratic education means stretching each child's mind to its own outer limits without injury to mental or physical health.

Fortunately growing interest in the gifted at school is helping sharpen public concern for the individualities of *all* children. Differentiated education is beginning to replace procrustean education, and fewer people are making a fetish of averageness in the normal curve. Yet, this new awareness that "sameness" and "equality" are *not* synonymous terms when they refer to educational opportunity has not always led to a clear understanding of existing knowledge in the field. A great many myths have masqueraded as truisms, and they tend to be reinforced rather than exploded in some of the awareness rallies, lectures, and workshops on behalf of gifted children. Even the professional literature has been affected by unsubstantiated claims about the nature and nurture of giftedness and by rhetoric that appeals more to the emotions than to reason.

It is time that some clearer impressions were recorded about the "state of the art" in understanding and educating the gifted in order to counterbalance some of the distortions, wishful thinking, overblown claims, and misdirected evangelism that has plagued the field. The intention of this Teachers College series of original monographs is to contribute to that kind of corrective. It has grown out of a federally supported contract to develop information products on key topics pertaining to the gifted and to bring them to the attention of the general public, including laymen and professionals. The authors have devoted considerable care to the content of their statements and the consequent impact on readers. Each writer is eminently qualified to make a balanced, meaningful contribution that avoids simply paraphrasing what others have said earlier. The aim is to inform through cogent presentations that can be appreciated by the widest possible audience ranging from those who want to be initiated to those who seek new insights into the field of educating the gifted.

Abraham J. Tannenbaum
Teachers College, Columbia University

REACHING OUT: ADVOCACY FOR THE GIFTED AND TALENTED

JONATHAN, A FIFTH-GRADE black boy who has never been out of his ghetto neighborhood, is described by his teachers as very outgoing, a born leader, enthusiastic, and bubbling with interests. On standardized tests he ranks in the upper one percent of the population. The school he attends, however, concentrates on teaching slow learners and bringing them "up to the norm." The staff expects that almost all the students will end their education after high school, unless they drop out before graduation. All but one or two of the teachers say they have "no time" to help students such as Jonathan study advanced topics.

Susan, in ninth grade, has had almost perfect marks since she entered public school. She has also been making pictures of all sorts—sketches, paintings, drawings, and more—since she discovered paper. Right now she prefers quick line drawings, which she even doodles on her dinner napkin. Her works have won prizes in local contests, and several local art teachers are eager to take her on as a special student. She hopes to enroll in such a special class. Her school offers her little opportunity to develop or display her talents. Her school principal feels that art instruction is nothing more than a costly frill.

Lynn, in high school, has been interested in science and math since her early years in school. She scores in the top 2 percent of her school on achievement tests and has participated on the school's math team. Lynn worries about the only chemistry teacher's strongly stated reluctance to having her in a laboratory course. Lynn was born with congenital cataracts and glaucoma. Despite her weakened perception, Lynn has excellent mobility skills and has learned to use several tactile and auditory aids for her studies.

Tom entered the ninth grade with a ranking in the top two percent of the population on standardized tests. In class though, Tom rarely concentrates on the work at hand, preferring instead to gaze out the window, draw complicated geometric designs in his notebook, or, at times, even create a disturbance that disrupts the class. Consequently Tom's teachers consider him a slow learner and assign him work that is suited for students two or three years younger than he. Not challenged by such tasks, Tom continues to be an underachiever.

Jonathan, Susan, Lynn, and Tom are but four of the nation's one and one-half to two and one-half million gifted and talented children found in schools from kindergarten through grade 12. Exceptional capacities create problems for most students, even at the earliest ages. Kindergarten children, as a whole, are reported by teachers to have the highest incidence of poor peer relationships, because they lack experience in adapting to requirements and in coping with frustrations and have far fewer available substitute activities than older pupils have. Young gifted children encounter difficulties in attempting to manage and direct activities. Since their ideas differ, they lose out in participating with others and find themselves marginal and isolated. Yet studies (Gallagher, 1975) show that gifted elementary school children rate high in popularity among their peers (p. 39).

The gifted tend to explore ideas and issues earlier than their peers. While they enjoy making friends as others do, they often tend to relate to older companions and to prefer games that involve some skill or intellectual pursuit. The gifted child is not necessarily a "grind" or a "loner," despite the fact that he or she develops special interests early. Biographical data of the gifted on a widespread basis reveal that they characteristically perform in an outstanding fashion—not only in individual pursuits but in widely varied organizations, such as community groups, student government, and athletics. The overall impression is of individuals who perform superbly in many fields and do so with ease.

Gifted pupils, even when very young, depart from self-centered concerns and values far earlier than their chronological peers. Interest in problems of morality, religion, society, and world peace is common even in elementary-age gifted children. Studies ranging from childhood to adults (Goldberg, 1965) indicate that the gifted value independence, are often more interested in the task or contribution at hand than recognition, prize integrity and independent judgment in decision making, reject conformity for its own sake, and possess unusually high social ideals and values.

Of all human groups, the gifted and talented are the least likely to form stereotypes. Their traits, interests, capacities, and alternatives present limitless possibilities for expression; the chief impression one draws from studying this group, at either the child or adult level, is of almost unlimited versatility, multiple talents, and countless ways of effective expression.

Considering the complex profile of this group, it is no simple task to define what makes a youngster gifted or talented. Some young people with potential mask their abilities in order to adapt to a more mundane group; others cannot find an outlet for their particular talents in a school setting. Many teachers and administrators turn a blind eye on a very bright child, even when talent is evident. The infinite variety within the population itself is a challenge; to be gifted is to be different and unique—and, too often, invisible.

Generally, however, the following evidence would indicate special intellectual gifts or talents:

• Consistently very superior scores on many appropriate standardized tests.

- •Demonstration of advanced skills, imaginative insight, and intense interest and involvement.
- •Judgment of teachers, administrators, supervisors, and specialists in various fields, including the arts, who are familiar with the abilities and potential of the individual and are qualified to evaluate them.

The Commissioner of Education (Marland, 1972) has defined gifted and talented children for purposes of federal education programs as follows:

Gifted and talented children are those identified by professional qualified persons who by virtue of outstanding abilities are capable of high performance. These are children who require differentiated educational services and/or programs beyond those normally provided by the regular school program in order to realize their contribution to self and society.

Children capable of high performance include those with demonstrated achievement and/or potential ability in any of the following areas, singly or in combination:

1. general intellectual ability
2. specific academic aptitude
3. creative or productive thinking
4. leadership ability
5. visual or performing arts
6. psychomotor ability.(p. 10)

HOW SHOULD THE GIFTED BE SERVED?

Research studies on the special needs of the gifted and talented demonstrate (Marland, 1972, p. 16) the need for special programs. Contrary to widespread belief, many of these students cannot excel without assistance. The relatively few gifted students who have had the advantage of special programs have shown remarkable improvement in self-understanding and in ability to relate well to others, as well as in improved academic and creative performance. The programs have not produced arrogant, selfish snobs; rather, special programs have extended a sense of reality, wholesome humility, self-respect, and respect for others. A good program for the gifted increases the involvement and interest in learning through the reduction of the irrelevant and redundant. This is not intended to imply that a "track system" for the gifted and talented is necessary but to show why it is that public schools are held responsible for providing programs for the gifted.

AN APPROACH TO ADVOCACY

When advocates for the gifted consider the ways in which they can have an impact on the educational institutions that service these students, they look at approaches that have been used over the past decades with varying degrees of success.

The traditional approach has been through parent-teacher associations. In the late sixties another mode became fashionable—the hastily organized emotional protest of a crowd united solely by their anger over some local development. A more recent way is through representation on an advisory committee established and controlled by the administrators of special programs. Whatever value these methods have in special cases, none has provided advocates for the gifted with a consistently effective means for moving schools and staff toward improved programs for the gifted.

While in some instances parents of the gifted have worked effectively through parent-teacher association committees, their actions are inevitably curtailed by the restrictions of the organization's constitution. No parent-teacher association can seem to favor a particular group of students over the school population as a whole. The adversary stance of emotional protest, because it is based upon the action of a group drawn together by a particular, often momentary crisis, does not provide effective means for establishing a stable and continuing relationship with a district staff or school board. Finally, the advisory committee, because its nonschool members are given only information deemed necessary by the administrators, has also proven ineffective. Only partially informed and made passive by their limited role, advocates on these committees find little opportunity to produce improvements in programs.

So it is necessary that those concerned with the education of gifted students seek other alternatives. One is what might be called *organized persuasion*. This concept does not exclude any of the useful elements of the other approaches. Indeed, it contains them because it is based on an open ended, flexible notion of effective action. It can perhaps be best defined as attempting to establish unassailable reasons for or against a course of conduct. And it has the advantage of being independent.

Organized persuasion becomes possible when a community of advocates reaches a consensus regarding important issues. But consensus is not enough. It requires force and direction, which is achieved by careful organization and by having a substantial number of people within the group who are willing to participate actively in pursuing its goals. At the same time, by organizing, the advocacy group is prepared to move beyond the first step, the resolution of tensions, to a constructive prescription for action.

The advocacy group has now institutionalized consensus. It is this organizing of opinion that enables interested women and men to become, as a group, a force in a community. A coherent body of citizens who advances persuasive arguments carries more weight than isolated individuals doing the same thing. It presents a businesslike face that authorities must take seriously, whether the intention is to move a district to action or to influence legislators to support specific provisions for gifted education within their districts or states. And when sympathetic policy makers are identified, the organization is there, ready to present them with substantial workable proposals to further the education of the gifted. These proposals, clearly thought out and offered in convincing form, enable policy makers to see ways of improving present offerings for gifted students.

THE WAY TO CONSENSUS

But how is consensus reached? What are the pitfalls to avoid? Anyone at all familiar with those interested in the future of gifted children is well aware that he or she is in the presence of a variety of strong independent opinions. Before any action for gifted students can be undertaken, it is necessary for advocates to focus on the question, "How can we do something constructive for the gifted?"

If positive action is to be taken, then parents, who make up from 40 percent to as high as 85 percent of advocacy groups,* have to resist the temptation to gather together merely for the purpose of exchanging "horror stories." These are often a substitute for becoming more actively involved. Advocates must also subdue the desire to rise up in righteous indignation and fling strident accusations of incompetence at the system. Attacking an administrator or teacher may relieve personal frustration, but it rarely leads to constructive problem solving. Some parents, who insist they don't want their children singled out for special attention, complain, both in public and in private, that the schools are wholly failing to educate their children. If what they say is really true, why aren't they applying themselves to remedy such a deplorable situation? Such an attitude often does produce results—negative results. It can infect their children with contempt for teachers and for learning generally. Ironically, their attitudes can have precisely the reverse effect of what they intend; discontented and contemptuous children are a problem in a classroom and may be singled out for special attention. The only difference is that the singling out has nothing to do with learning.

Horror story telling obviously goes nowhere, since it isn't directed outside the story circle. Vituperation and complaint, if they become aggravating enough, do arouse school boards and administrations to one of two kinds of response, both of which seek to quiet the rage but rarely address the real problems. One is to prescribe placebos in the form of "special" field trips or "fun and games" frills. The other is to encourage the common belief that gifted children are either figments of neurotic parents' fantasies or "will make it anyhow."

Recrimination, complaint, and horror stories may be enough to satisfy some, but they do not address the heart of the matter. Such attitudes have to yield in favor of thinking through what a good gifted program should be and what can be done to ensure that such a program has a chance of thriving in a particular setting.

A consensus of negative opinion is easy enough to gather. What is needed is consensus on a plan of action, a coming together of advocates dedicated to develop-

---

*From a summary report based on a questionnaire study developed by the American Association for Gifted Children in 1978.

ing a serious strategy that speaks reasonably and persuasively to the apathy or hostility of policy makers.

TAKE A LOOK AT THE OPTIONS

Existing educational opportunities for the gifted vary, depending on what a state or school district have available. According to the circumstances, each advocacy group must decide where it can best direct its attention. Whether it is the state legislature, the county board of trustees, the local school district, or an independent institution such as a lyceum, the campaign strategy must direct its arguments to the right audience.

For example, if a group agrees that a statewide specific legal and financial commitment is needed before anything else, then it must prepare to work with state legislators. This strategy requires that a number of local groups throughout the state work together. Arguments should stress that meeting the needs of gifted students is part of the state's legal responsibility to educate all students according to their abilities. Presenting such arguments means traveling to the state capitol and engaging the interest and support of key legislators, particularly members of education and finance committees. In the beginning, arguments are usually presented in conversation and small group exchange. More formal presentations should wait for an appropriate setting. While it is necessary to contact members of key committees, it is also wise to seek out the state representatives of the local areas of the groups participating. What do they think about education generally and education for the gifted particularly? Most people in government have strong opinions on the subject of education. Since the object is to influence opinion in the direction one wants it to go, the arguments must be effective.

If the county is the target of organized persuasion, a group representing a number of its districts is the most persuasive. The county approach is particularly suited to rural or sparsely populated areas where centralized direction and funding are needed to improve program offerings for the gifted. Good will results from sharing the opportunities for the gifted as well as the burden of funding. The board of trustees, the county superintendent, and any special education departments can be avenues to explore. If the initial effort produces a mobile resource center for the gifted that serves teachers, parents, and students on a rotating basis, possibilities for developing programs further are more apt to occur.

Usually, however, a group decides to direct its effort on the local district level. This is understandable, since it is the children closest to us that we are most immediately concerned with. But as success in one district often stimulates activity in another, the scope of advocacy involvement may gradually grow to include the county and state.

In a district with no offerings for the gifted, there is a special problem. What can be found on which to build a gifted program? Without the help of any framework established by the district or the state, advocates of the gifted may begin by trying to influence decisions concerning general curriculum. By exploring this possibility in a constructive, cooperative manner, they may help to develop a nucleus of offerings open enough to allow gifted students to really learn without demanding that any teacher establish two mutually exclusive curricula. When such areas of curriculum, preferably in core academic courses, have been identified, parents are likely to find both teachers and administrators who are amenable to change. If professionals are met with good will and cooperation, they will respond in kind. There are few good educators today who do not welcome any help they can get in improving what schools can do for all students.

If none of these options for working through public institutions seems to be available, a group may decide that it has to begin outside public education. Advocates tend to feel—perhaps rightly—that this course is an admission of defeat not just for themselves, but for public education in general. And if a group does not establish goals that move it beyond this course, the defeat must be laid in large measure at the feet of advocates themselves.

As a first step, working outside the schools can increase the visibility of the gifted in the eyes of educators and policy makers. For example, Saturday classes or summer programs designed for gifted children have been offered at community colleges. Independent lyceums have also been established, involving interested members of a community—doctors, lawyers, artists, business people, and even concerned educators, to name a few. Neither program is necessarily academic, but both offer something beyond the average curriculum. In both these cases, however, tuition is necessary, either as a charge per class in the community college or as dues for membership in the lyceum, and students must assume the costs for books and materials.

How do these programs raise the visibility of gifted children? The enthusiasm of both the students and their teachers, who may be community volunteers, communicates itself to the whole community. Student displays, art shows, demonstrations, and performances can be shared with the public. The accomplishments of young people always delight, and often amaze, adults. Such programs also generate questions about the adequacy of an educational system that fails to provide equally challenging activities.

Such programs, however, should be viewed as short-term activities directed to the long-range goal—to persuade a district to meet the needs of the gifted students in its jurisdiction. By presenting a variety of teaching styles and curricula outside the schools, the advocacy group suggests thoughtful and exciting alternatives to the narrow range of a standard curriculum. But care must be taken that these programs are not viewed by the schools as relieving them of their responsibility to the gifted. If this happens, the very intention of such an undertaking is defeated.

A WARNING ABOUT EXPECTATIONS

Here a word of caution is necessary. Expectations are as important as identi-fying the route to take. Boundless ambition can destroy any enterprise. Persuading people to change their minds and to adopt new policies are slow and difficult pro-cesses. Often members of an advocacy organization are so convinced of the rightness of their position that they are unprepared to cope with resistance, or out-right hostility, to those arguments that they may encounter. Wringing their hands, they cry "What's the use?" or shrug and say, "What else can you expect from those bureaucrats?" Both questions are rhetorical; neither requires nor receives an an-swer.

A modest start with modest expectations is almost always best. It promises at least some chance of success. Trying to change the entire curriculum or restruc-ture the administration or rewrite the education code invites certain disaster. There really isn't any "establishment" to change; there are only individuals, some with habits of mind flexible enough to consider alternatives, others too rigid to con-template change. Of course, there is legislation to be written or programs to be developed, but these changes come only through moving individuals to act.

Some people in a position to assist advocacy efforts will be venturesome enough to experiment. But they will want to work for change in an atmosphere of cooperation. If an advocacy organization gains their help, it can afford to overlook others who hesitate out of fear or laziness. The latter will take their cues from the leaders.

If a few teachers, administrators, or legislators are persuaded that the argued position makes sense, a beginning has been made. And that should be enough to hope for at first. In getting that far, significant progress has been made. There are others out there who will pick up and carry the message further. From then on, it is a matter of taking time to consider every step carefully, asking if it will bring the results desired. For example, who in each instance is the audience to be addressed? What can it actually accomplish? What should it be persuaded to do? People cannot respond usefully in areas where they have no influence. If the action desired is unrealistic, the result is bound to be disappointing.

Organized persuasion is not an instant panacea; it is a continuing process to influence those who can effect change. And change occurs when such people are convinced that each development grows naturally out of what has preceded it. It takes time to develop, and it takes even more time to grow into that final goal, a consensus shared by the advocacy group and the public school system alike. An independent and responsible advocacy organization can be a great asset to teach-ers, administrators, and legislators in the evolution of this whole process.

Finally, an advocacy organization must have some notion of the expectations of the people on the other side of the table. Do they view the organization's repre-sentatives as reasonable negotiators? If not, they cannot take the organization seriously. Arguing persuasively means providing those to be influenced with important or new information, organized, not as a catalog of unrelated facts, but as an argument with clear conclusions and concrete proposals subscribed to by a constituency. If they come to expect this, they will listen. If sometimes they pay more attention to the manner of presentation than the actual material, the end result is the same; they will have heard from the organization, and if the presentation is forceful, clear, and available in written form, they will have a chance to mull over the position in quieter, private moments, free of the public pressure that inspires defensive reactions.

MOVING BEYOND THE ADVERSARY POSITION

But how do the suggestions of an advocacy group become institutionalized on the local district level? It is discontent, undeniably deep, if often unspecified, that usually provides the stimulus to form an advocacy group—certainly this is true in the area of gifted education—and discontent, accompanied by controversy, naturally puts the group in an adversary position. Such a position often results in improving conditions for gifted students. With success, however, the adversary posture becomes obsolete. Yet it is likely to seem, through sheer habit, the only policy to fall back on unless the organization has considered what it wishes to do next. Organizations that want to remain effective are faced with the necessity of adjusting their position to a changed set of circumstances.

Though the conditions for controversy may still remain—for example, the recalcitrance of administrators and the hostility of teachers—organizations must be prepared to support staff who are developing programs. Advocacy groups should be able to discriminate between minor issues, usually surfacing at individual schools, and the major need to establish stable policies of overall cooperation in support of programs for the gifted. If the issue that initiated the organization of an advocacy group required a strong aggressive position, the group's long-term strategy will require thoughtful flexibility. Advocates cannot afford to freeze in a stance that does not meet, for example, the altered need to sustain or advance a newly established program. A rigid reliance on the adversary posture can damage an organization's effectiveness and even undermine the position gained for gifted students. However, if subsequently an issue does arise that calls for stronger action, an organization that has demonstrated its good will has earned the right to anger and is in a good position to use it.

Flexibility, however, does not mean abandonment of standards; it does mean that organizations must avoid crises that militate against program development. This condition is only possible if there is trust between parents and educators. Developing trust depends, in part, on recognizing where the legitimate areas of advocate involvement end and staff responsibility begins. Advocacy has little effect where advocates are unwilling to recognize such boundaries. Understanding the intention of the program, as viewed by the professionals, also enhances the ability to bring about change in areas of fundamental disagreement. It is always necessary to keep the door open for dialogue between the organization and staff for the gifted.

The administrative and fiscal responsibilities for school programs belong in the domain of the program director and staff. Giving them cooperative support will encourage them to turn to the advocacy group for suggestions regarding goals and objectives. Directors who don't include parents or other outsiders in their planning may be either arrogant or frightened. If they are responding solely to the adversary stance of a group, it may point to a weakness of the advocacy organization. It is up to the latter to map out a common ground where both sides can work comfortably together without either side losing face.

Final school decisions are made by school professionals. Advocacy groups that understand this fact avoid postures that attack their legitimate authority and lead to hostility, if not paralysis. It often allows the higher administration to explain the law and remain neutral, rejoicing that they have contained another disturbance —and still doing nothing for gifted students. While advocates can do much to ensure a successful program, no program is even possible without the school professionals' skills. This does not mean that advocates or parents need to become rubber stamps. They can assist the staff in tasks that are necessary to a successful program without losing their right to question decisions when that need arises.

A balance then has to be maintained that weighs fairly between parent conviction and the practical knowledge of educators, a balance achieved by working closely together on all matters, with a steady eye toward the students and their growth. The objective detachment of a teacher must be given its due, as must the conviction of advocates. Both parties must learn to respect each other's capacity to contribute. But respect means sympathetic honesty, not uncritical mutual admiration. Where staff has the right to criticize advocates for indulging their egos, advocates have the right to criticize staff for thinking more about public relations than about public education. When these mutual rights are granted by both parties, advocates can influence major decisions, staff can respond to constructive criticism, and children profit from the results.

FUTURE OF THE ORGANIZATION

After the first aims are won, what, then, does the organization do? Is an organization's usefulness ended when its efforts result in an identifiable, funded program for the gifted? By no means. Whether mandated by district policy or state law, a program for the gifted can still suffer neglect. An independent advocacy organization can serve as a deterrent to the diminution of programs at higher levels of administration. It can provide community support for teachers and program directors in their struggle to maintain quality. So many other urgent and reasonable pressures are being brought to bear on school systems by a variety of advocacy groups that gifted education requires continuous support.

The gap between mandated programs and implementation is often a chasm. There are a large number of "paper programs" for the gifted that have no reality beyond lip service, yet they permit institutions to receive monies meant, but not used, for the gifted. Here organized advocacy can play a watchdog role, both in bringing these discrepancies to the administration's attention and in providing suggestions to remedy problems. Carrying such a stick, the advocacy group should tread carefully. It should support the program's objectives as stated, if it can, or provide constructive suggestions for alterations to the program director for her or his consideration, perhaps as is often done by establishing an advisory board to meet regularly with the director.

Advocacy generally centers on two essential areas—the program of studies and the funding. The program, usually considered first and most important by many, is viewed in relation to the district's curriculum development. The more integral the program is to general curriculum, the greater will be its strength. The program is the very heart of gifted education, and when it is properly developed and realized, it earns the support of parents, educators, policy makers, and taxpayers. It is a visible manifestation justifying present and future support. Ultimately the form and effectiveness of programs for the gifted reflect the quality and level of a district's general curriculum offerings, particularly in academic courses.

Of course, it is impossible to address the whole educational design of a local district, but it is possible to identify the most glaring gaps for gifted students in a district's curriculum and to work to solve them. Thus, general curriculum is a legitimate and necessary area of concern to advocates for the gifted.

The other center of interest is funds. Funds earmarked for gifted programs may be used only for staff and materials that, in the general program, would not be provided otherwise for gifted students; such funds should be so coded in a district's total budget. Advocacy organizations need to press for a separate category, clearly showing the budget for the gifted within the overall budget. The aim is to make it possible to watch at key points how gifted funds are spent. When put in their own category rather than included in general funds, gifted-alloted monies are less prone to be lost.

When the law governing the use of funds for the gifted is not observed, a district may be penalized or lose the monies entirely, as well as its program too. Awareness of the ins and outs of financial accountability can be of great value to an advocacy group in securing proper uses of monies for the gifted. It can also spark a campaign for gifted handicapped children who are entitled to special programs beyond those serving their handicap.

When organized persuasion has raised awareness of the educational needs of the gifted and helped develop or strengthen genuine programs for them, the task is far from done. Situations continually change and can imperil all the hard-won accomplishments of the past. No achievement is perfect; there is always room for improvement. An organization must stay alive to these possibilities. On the larger scene, new laws or amendments will be needed as more gifted students are located and programs continue to expand. As long as there are gifted children, there will be a need for advocates organized to protect and improve their education. And as long as those in authority are susceptible to reason, organized persuasion will be the best method to attain these ends.

GETTING READY

Organizing a group of advocates for the gifted isn't easy. The basic steps of setting up an organization, appointing the committees needed, and holding the first meeting give an idea of what's ahead.

I. Select a person to act as coordinator of all efforts and to chair a steering committee. Name an acting treasurer who will be a member of the steering committee, as well as acting chairpersons of the following committees to develop plans and be responsible for specific jobs needed to be done in starting an association.

   a. A bylaws committee of three or more persons should be selected to develop suggested bylaws for the organization. Copies of bylaws of other associations may be used as guides (see Appendix for a sample).

   b. A program committee should be selected to find and recommend program resources in the area. These resources may include local administrative personnel, other educators, interested professional and business people, and staff from colleges or universities. Include all possible means to inform members regarding the needs of the gifted (psychological, social, educational, and the like) as well as the laws and policies within which the schools have to work to meet the needs of gifted students.

   c. A publicity committee should be selected to organize the use of every avenue of publicity in the community. Local press, radio, and television should be given written information regarding the organization, meeting places, time, program, and plans. Posters can be placed in libraries, businesses, and other areas. Publicity about programs should be continuous, starting with the need for them, the beginning of pilot programs, and persistent coverage of established or expanding programs.

   d. A hospitality committee should be appointed to plan the development of a spirit of friendliness within the group. Both men and women should be on the committee. Serving coffee or other simple refreshments is helpful to encourage interaction of those in attendance.

   e. Membership committee

      1. This committee should have materials available to accept payment of

membership dues at the first meeting, as soon as bylaws (which include amount of dues) are accepted. Dues payments may be effectively handled by having at hand a short form indicating name, address, city, zip code, home and office telephones, and a place to check status as parent, educator, or other. A check or cash could be attached by the person joining, and the process can be handled quickly.

2. A questionnaire should be developed to reveal the interests and skills of members who may volunteer to serve on various committees. Maximum effort should be made to involve all interested persons.

3. A community-resources form should be developed for the purpose of encouraging persons in attendance to offer available learning experiences to the gifted. This could be an opportunity to find hidden talents in homemakers and hobbyists, in addition to professionals and businesses.

4. This committee should plan to conduct a membership drive with the help of the publicity committee and the school administration.

f. Public affairs committee. Cooperating with local school officials, this committee should meet with school board members, school superintendent, director of special education, director of instruction, director of psychological testing, and any other personnel who might be involved with services to the gifted. Members should become knowledgeable about school programs and what can be done within the restrictions of laws and policy and through the use of local, state, and federal funds. The committee can encourage the use of funds in ways that are meaningful to the children in the community and keep the membership informed of needs and potential concerns.

II. Establish a date, time, and place for a public meeting, select a program of interest, have the publicity committee utilize all avenues to inform the public, and see that the other committees are ready to function.

At the first meeting it would be well to adopt bylaws to formalize the organization. A break should be planned for payment of dues and completion of membership information. The amount of dues will have just been democratically decided upon with the adoption of the bylaws. Officers may be elected to the executive board at the first organizational meeting, or a nominating committeee may be elected to nominate officers at the next meeting. The steering committee should continue to be in charge of meetings until officers are elected and installed. Each candidate for office or on the nominating committee should be a member of the association with current dues paid, and his or her consent should be obtained before the nomination is made. Officers should represent various areas and interests in the community and be dedicated to the gifted. Since gifted children and youth are found in all socioeconomic, cultural, and ethnic groups, it is very important to focus on a democratic organization from the start and to avoid projecting an elitist image.

Apply for an Internal Revenue Service business number so that the group can benefit from being a not-for-profit, tax-exempt organization (see Appendix for sample letters).

KEEPING THE ORGANIZATION ALIVE

The long-term success of your organization will depend on both the quality and quantity of members personally involved in the work of the group. People have varying degrees of ability and time to take leadership or supportive roles.

It is the responsibility of the officers and chairpersons to see that the maximum possible number of members have a "piece of the action" and are given the opportunity to grow in capability and interest. Members' commitments of time and talents to the organization depend on the acceptance and challenge of the leadership. Sometimes a leader feels that it would take less time and energy to "do it himself" than to find someone else to guide. However, developing other people's ability to participate and encouraging their commitment to the group effort expands the scope of an organization.

It must be remembered that involvement in an advocate organization has degrees of commitment; that is, there will be those, usually few in number, who are willing to devote a great deal of time and energy to the work involved in changing the attitudes of educators and legislators. The larger part of the membership will be made up of those who wish to be involved only on special occasions when a show of solidarity is needed, or even more narrowly, when they can be reasonably assured that their efforts will meet with success. They will come to a school board meeting when the subject of gifted education is being considered, or if such a program's existence is being threatened; they may even publicly express their support for the program, but they will consider that having done that, they have done all they need to do.

There is in our society a deeply ingrained timidity before the authority of educators. No one wants to be suspected of meddling or favoring some children over others. These attitudes act as strong deterrents to interested women and men to engage in the kind of prolonged activity that good organization work demands. But for those undaunted few, who have the toughness to endure and are supported by the results of consensus, the tool of organized persuasion can make meaningful dialogue possible.

No organization should be content to have only one person who does all the work, all the persuading, and all the decision making. When this happens, the organization forfeits the first requirements of organized persuasion—consensus. Particularly in the public arena, putting all affairs in the hands of one active participant, no matter how effective that person may be, will cost an advocate group its validity in the minds of those it desires to influence. They will no longer see it as such-and-such an organization but as so-and-so's clique.

When this happens, both the organization and the individual lose their effectiveness. The individual, often unintentionally, usurps powers that belong rightfully to the organization. It is virtually impossible for an individual shouldering total responsibility not to feel responsible for all decisions. Subtly the role changes from leader to boss, and the first resistance to the boss's decisions leads to conflict. Total power in one place erodes the very flexibility that can make a body based on organized persuasion so beautifully able to deal with changing circumstances.

The governing board of an organization should be made up of individuals who are all willing to share duties. Otherwise the organization may be left with a serious gap if one member has to drop out. The board also requires some regular turnover in its composition so that new and alternative possibilities can have a hearing.

Committee planning can contribute toward a strong organization. Care should be taken to see that any plan submitted has been well thought out with detailed plans of action, costs, and financing before being brought to the executive board for approval. The time and action of the executive board should not be expended on filling gaps in a committee's planning but on evaluating its recommendations.

Checklists of committees and the work to be done should be distributed at meetings so that all members have the opportunity and are encouraged to become participants. Committee chairpersons have the obligation to give those who offer to help an opportunity to join in committee planning and functioning.

Do not be depressed if the organization starts with only a few people. The group will grow and be able to serve more and more gifted students as the word spreads to others who are seeking better services for these students. The goal is to find all gifted and talented children and to help them develop their potential.

Don't be an "only." Your child is one among many, and you will find others "out there" seeking the same goals and creative solutions.

GOING STATEWIDE

A state organization is a vital agent in forming cohesive leadership for the gifted and talented. Constant communication between a local group, state leaders, and other local groups is the only way to have a real "handle" on effecting change to improve opportunities and facilities for these special students.

Each group can learn much from others—and put it together in state leadership for all. Local school policies and programming must mesh with state school policies and guidelines. Decisions made locally are affected by decision makers from all over the state. Any group is limited in its ability to obtain maximum and continuing services for gifted and talented students unless it works on a statewide basis.

Membership will grow statewide by asking advocates in various areas of the state to recommend others who might be interested in working for the cause and by addressing various groups about what can be accomplished by organizing statewide.

Also consider these activities:

- Send articles to all news media in the state, including daily, neighborhood, and weekly newspapers and television and radio stations, telling about the identification and needs of the gifted and the availability of opportunities for organization membership.
- Send posters, including information about the association and its address, to all public libraries in the state with the request that they be placed on bulletin boards both in general areas of the library and in the children's departments. Lists of libraries may usually be obtained from the state department of education.
- Ask local school administrations' directors of instruction to assist in finding leadership to organize chapters. Or a search among the people who respond to the first two promotion activities may turn up leadership.

In addition to carrying out responsibilities outlined in the bylaws, members of a state governing board should be missionaries to help in organizing chapters, finding leaders, and furnishing resources for various committees of the chapters. Members who have been outstanding in taking responsibility in the chapters should be brought into the state leadership.

The publicity chairperson should work closely with the membership chairperson to develop informative articles for all news media in the state, always including information about contacting the state association. Subjects for articles could include characteristics of gifted and talented students, opportunities available to them throughout the state and nation, and specific activities of the state association.

The public affairs chairperson should become familiar with the state laws, funding (on-going or potential), policies, procedures, personnel involved, and how these mesh with the local school policies and potentials. Continuing information regarding developments in the state department of education, the legislature, or other state offices should be given to both chapters and individual members. The chairperson should work with chapter public affairs chairpersons and interested others to keep the membership informed regarding governmental developments for the gifted and talented.

A program chairperson should develop resources and ideas for interesting and relevant programs and projects that may be used by chapters and the state association.

A newsletter editor should develop a regular communication that goes to all members. Information regarding happenings in chapters and the state, opportunities throughout the nation for the gifted and talented, reports of conferences, and research should be reported to membership. Such a communication can develop interested and informed members.

The officers of the association should plan and implement an annual convention. The convention should include:

- A business meeting
- Training and resources for local chapter officers, chairpersons, and members
- Highlights of school programming in the state
- Planned program and participation of children—preschool through high school
- Happenings on the national level
- National professional and research developments
- State and national opportunities available for the gifted and talented.

Cooperation with the state department of education personnel assigned to the gifted and talented program can be a tremendous asset in planning and implementing a convention.

THE STORY OF ONE NATIONAL ADVOCACY ORGANIZATION— THE AMERICAN ASSOCIATION FOR GIFTED CHILDREN

Each advocate organization has its own history and development, depending on the people who created and support it. The American Association for Gifted Children, the first voluntary organization devoted exclusively to the gifted, was founded in New York City, in 1946. Two women with varied experience in education and a group of their friends from various fields and professions were concerned about the great neglect and abuse of gifted youngsters.

To promote the interests of the gifted over the years, the Association has published many materials. Its book, *The Gifted Child*, a first of its kind, was published in 1951. More recently, in 1978, the Association prepared a new volume entitled, *On Being Gifted*, in which 20 gifted youths, drawn from all levels of society, tell what it feels like to be gifted. The second part of the book discusses useful alternatives in their education. A new book, *The Gifted Child, the Family, and the Community*, is in preparation. A series of recently revised bulletins, *Guideposts*, representing a coordinated approach to parents, teachers, administrators, and young people themselves, are available. In addition to publishing, the Association members participate in conferences on the national, state and local level. The Association has formed a joint committee with the American Library Association to work cooperatively on ways in which the gifted can be served by both groups. As a result, ALA's magazine, *Top of the News,* ran a 50-page spread on "Library Service to the Gifted" in November 1971. The joint committee has also prepared a folder, *The Library Is My Best Friend,* which is distributed by both organizations.

The AAGC has also cooperated with the National Association of Secondary School Principals, which carried in the March 1976 issue of its *Bulletin* an article on the gifted prepared by the Association's members.

The AAGC administers the Mary Jane and Jerome A. Straka Scholarship, which provides assistance for high school graduates particularly interested in the areas of business, math, and science. The Association has also cooperated with the Van Pelt Foundation in sponsoring college scholarships and summer study programs at eastern colleges for gifted young Native Americans. The organization has from time to time sponsored programs of art scholarships, in consultation with the National Arts Club and the U.S. Office of Education, to assist young people who would benefit from further study within the art field. Additional matching funds are being sought to continue these scholarships, to expand them to junior high school students, and to cover the fields of music, dance, architecture, graphic arts, and literature.

The AAGC participated in the organization and development of Project BRIDGE, a career education program for gifted high school students, developed in the Yonkers, New York, public schools. It has also sponsored a study, developed in Wisconsin, entitled "Rural Delinquency Proneness: Its Relationship to Giftedness, Environmental Support, and Environmental Availability."

These examples show the range of activities an advocacy organization may take in addition to promoting local school programs for the gifted.

APPENDIX: SAMPLE LOCAL ASSOCIATION DEVELOPMENT MATERIALS

FORMATION ANNOUNCEMENT

TO: Board of Education
Superintendent of Schools
School Principals
P. T. A. Presidents

SUBJECT: Association for the Academically Talented

This is to announce the formation of the (city, county) Association for the Academically Talented. Membership is open to anyone interested in furthering the purpose of the association, which is to encourage development of new and innovative programs for education of the gifted, to encourage educators and the general public to become acquainted with programs for the gifted at local, state, and federal levels, and to share that knowledge.

Any efforts for the gifted and talented will have our support, and we would appreciate it if you would inform concerned teachers and parents.

Name(s) of organizer(s)
Telephone number(s)

IRS TAX-EXEMPTION STATUS MATERIALS

TO: All Chapters of the (state name) Association for the Academically Talented,
      Inc.

We have obtained tax-exempt status with the Internal Revenue Service on a group
basis.

If you desire to be or continue to be a part of this group exemption, it is necessary
to sign and submit the enclosed letters:

　　　(A) Annual information for tax-exempt status report

　　　(B) Annual information for filing group return.

If you already have a Federal Employer Identification Number, please indicate it on
the letter. If not, complete and sign a SS-4 Form (complete top and bottom section).
For Item #7, check box marked "other" and after the box put "group exemption
request." For Box #10, use "Non-profit—educational." After your chapter name on
Line 1, write in "Affiliate of the ——— Association for the Academically Talented,
Inc." Mail completed SS-4 Form to Internal Revenue Service Center (local address).

                                          Sincerely,

                                          ———, President

Annual Group Filing Return

Central Organization
Address

Gentlemen:

The following information is submitted for filing a group return with the Internal Revenue Service:

1. Gross receipts from dues $
2. Gross receipts from other sources (identify) $
3. A brief summary of expenses paid $
4. Assets (in total) as of 9-1 $
5. Assets (in total) as of 8-31 $
6. Liabilities at 9-1 $
7. Liabilities at 8-31 $

By _____

(Title) _____

Telephone No. _____

Name of Chapter _____

_____

Street Address _____

_____ ZIP _____
City

DATED _____

Federal Employer Identification Number _____

Annual Tax-Exempt Status Report

Central Organization
Address

Gentlemen:

In order to comply with group exemption letter requirements under Section 501(c) (3) of the Internal Revenue Code for tax exemption purposes, we hereby attest to the following:

1. We are a subordinate or chapter of the (state) Association for the Academically Talented, Inc. (the central organization)

2. We are subject to general supervision or control by the central organization.

3. We agree to abide by the Constitution and By-laws (as amended) of the central organization.

4. We are eligible for exemption under the same Internal Revenue Code rulings.

5. We are not a private foundation.

6. Our activities and purposes are the same as the central organization.

7. We authorize our name to be added to the roster of the central organization.

By _____
President   •

Telephone No. _____

Name of Chapter _____

_____

Street Address _____

_____ ZIP _____
City

DATED _____

Federal Employer Identification Number _____

Applied for on _____ (Date) and will be sent when received.

SAMPLE CONSTITUTION
AND BYLAWS

ADOPTED _____

ARTICLE I.   NAME

Section 1.   The name of this organization shall be _____

_____

ARTICLE II.   PURPOSES

Section 1.   This shall be a non-profit organization formulated to create an awareness among parents, educators, legislature, and the general public of the needs of the gifted and talented.

Section 2.   To support development of the new and innovated programs for the gifted and talented.

Section 3.   To share knowledge of the educational programs at local, state, and federal levels.

Section 4.   To advocate state and federal legislation for the benefit of gifted and talented children and youths.

ARTICLE III.   MEMBERSHIP

Section 1.   Membership shall be open to all persons and organizations interested in the purposes listed in Article II.

Section 2.   Individuals and chapters interested in the objectives of this organization shall become members by donating yearly a minimum contribution determined by the executive board. Exemption from Federal income tax is under Section 501 (c) (3) of Internal Revenue Code of 1954. Group exemption number _____, Employer identification number (EIN) _____.

Section 3.   The membership year begins ___(month)___ and ends ___(month)___.

Section 4.   Each member shall be entitled one vote.

ARTICLE IV.   OFFICERS AND THEIR ELECTION

Section 1.   The officers of the Association shall be a President, Vice President, a Corresponding Secretary, a Recording Secretary, and a Treasurer.

Section 2.   Officers shall be elected at the annual meeting in the spring to take office the following __(month)__ .

Section 3.   At the expiration of his term of office, the President shall automatically become the Past President.

Section 4.   A vacancy occurring in any office shall be filled for the unexpired term by a member of the Association elected by a majority of the remaining members of the Executive Committee.

Section 5.   The term of office for each officer shall start __(month)__ following his election, except those elected in special elections who shall assume office at once.

ARTICLE V.   DUTIES OF OFFICERS

Section 1.   The President shall preside at all meetings of the Executive Committee and of the Association and shall perform all such duties assigned to him by the Executive Committee.

Section 2.   The Vice President shall act as an aid to the President, shall perform the duties of the President in the absence of that officer, and shall act as Program Chairperson of the Association.

Section 3.   The Recording Secretary shall record the minutes of all meetings of the Executive Committee and of the Association and shall perform other such duties as may be delegated by the President.

Section 4.   The Corresponding Secretary shall conduct the Correspondence of __(organization)__, send notices of __(organization)__ meetings to members, and perform other such duties as may be delegated by the President.

Section 5.   The Treasurer shall keep an accurate record of receipts and disbursements and shall make a full report at the annual meeting and serve as Membership Chairperson.

ARTICLE VI.   STANDING COMMITTEES

Section 1.   Standing Committees of the Association shall be the Executive Committee, the Membership Committee, the Program Committee, the Liaison and Affiliation Committee, the Nominating Committee, the Legislative Committee, and the Auditing Committee.

Section 2.   Executive Committee
a.   The Executive Committee shall consist of the officers of the Association, the immediate Past President, and the Chairpersons of the Standing Committees.
b.   The Executive Committee shall be empowered to act for the Association between general membership meetings.
c.   A quorum of the Executive Committee shall be a majority of the Committee.

Section 3.   The Membership Committee shall consist of a chairperson who shall be the Treasurer and members of the Association selected by the chairperson. The chairperson shall receive monies for membership dues made payable to the ___ (organization)___.

Section 4.   The Program Committee shall consist of a chairperson who shall be the Vice President and members of the Association selected by the chairperson.

Section 5.   The Liaison and Affiliation Committee shall consist of a chairperson selected by the President and any other persons chosen by the chairperson. The Committee shall coordinate efforts between groups.

Section 6.   The Nominating Committee shall consist of a chairperson who shall be the immediate Past President. He shall select a committee of six members: three from the Executive Committee and three from the general membership. The slate of the Nominating Committee shall be sent to the membership in advance of the annual meeting or published in the newsletter.

Section 7.   The Publishing Committee shall consist of a chairperson selected by the President. Other members of the Committee shall be selected by its chairperson. This Committee shall be responsible for publishing the Newsletter and also brochures as designed by the Executive Committee.

Section 8.   The Auditing Committee shall consist of a chairperson selected by the President and any other members selected by the chairperson. The Committee shall audit the records of _____ annually in _____ and report to the general membership.

Section 9.

The Legislative Committee shall consist of a chairperson selected by the President and any other members selected by the chairperson. The Committee shall advocate state and federal legislation for the benefit of gifted and talented children.

Section 10.

The Executive Officers may establish ad hoc temporary committees whenever advisable and necessary to facilitate the purpose of the Association.

ARTICLE VII.

MEETINGS

Section 1.

There shall be a minimum of one general meeting during the school year.

Section 2.

Meetings shall be conducted by the duly elected officers of the Association.

Section 3.

There shall be a minimum of 2 Executive Committee meetings each year.

ARTICLE VIII.

PARLIAMENTARY AUTHORITY

Section 1.

The most recent publication of *Robert's Rules of Order* shall be the authority in all questions of parliamentary procedure.

ARTICLE IX.

AMENDMENTS AND REVISIONS

Section 1.

These by-laws may be amended by a majority of those present at any Association meeting. All members shall be notified in writing at least twenty (20) days previous to the meeting at which the vote on the matter will be taken.

ARTICLE X.

DISSOLUTION OF ASSOCIATION

Section 1.

In the event of dissolution, all assets, real and personal, shall be distributed to such organizations as are qualified as tax exempt under Section 501 (c) (3) of the Internal Revenue Code or the corresponding provisions of a future United States Internal Revenue Law.

SAMPLE MEETING AGENDA

_____

ORGANIZATION

_____

TYPE OF MEETING (Executive or general)

_____

DATE

_____

PLACE

AGENDA

1. Call to Order and Roll Call
2. Communications
3. Minutes from last meeting—corrections
4. Treasurer's report
5. Constitutional Amendment
6. Membership Report
7. Newsletter Report
8. Annual Meeting Report
9. Report from Chapters
10. Submitted proposal report
11. Logo
12. Awareness and promotional items—report
16. Issuance of Certificates of Merit for Annual Meeting
17. Other Business
18. Set next meeting date.
19. Adjournment

SAMPLE MINUTES FORM

Meeting: regular   special (reason)
Name of organization:
Time of meeting:
Place of meeting:
Called to order by:
Minutes of the previous meeting: read and accepted, read and amended, dis-
                        pensed with.

Guests:
Treasurer's report:
Standing committee reports: summarize or attach copies.
Special committee reports:
OLD BUSINESS:
1. Motion:
   Made by: Seconded by:
   Discussion for the motion:
   Against the motion:
   Passed: Rejected:
NEW BUSINESS:
1. Motion:
   Made by: Seconded by:
   Discussion for the motion:
   Against:
   Passed: Rejected:
UNFINISHED BUSINESS:
1. Motion:
   Made by: Seconded by:
   Discussion for the motion:
   Against:
   Passed: Rejected:
ANNOUNCEMENTS
1.
2.
3.
PROGRAM (A short description)
The next meeting will be: Place:
The meeting was adjourned at:
                        Sincerely submitted,
                        _____, Recording Secretary

ORGANIZATION RATING FORM

Evaluating your group is a must. Feedback from the group can let you know where you are. Look for answers to these questions:

1. How are we doing as a group?
2. Does everyone agree with what we are doing?
3. What did we do that was effective?
4. What mistakes did we make?
5. Have we a record of all our meetings?

The following type of questionnaire could be used to give you an idea about answering these questions. Try to reach via mail, telephone, or as a hand-out at meetings as many people as possible for the maximum input.

How Effective is Our Organization?

1. Do we have interesting, lively meetings?

   _____ Yes   _____ No   _____ Sometimes

2. Do we make everyone feel welcome?

   _____ Yes   _____ No   _____ Sometimes

3. Does everyone know everyone else's name?

   _____ Yes   _____ No   _____ Sometimes

4. Does everyone have a chance to talk?

   _____ Yes   _____ No   _____ Sometimes

5. Does everyone have a job to do?

   _____ Yes   _____ No   _____ Sometimes

6. Are the top jobs passed around?

   _____ Yes   _____ No   _____ Sometimes

7. Does everyone know what's going on?

   _____ Yes   _____ No   _____ Sometimes

8. Are the financial records open and understandable to all?

   _____ Yes   _____ No   _____ Sometimes

9. Are people effectively informed of meeting times and places?

   _____ Yes   _____ No   _____ Sometimes

10. Do we seem to have a plan of action?

    _____ Yes   _____ No   _____ Sometimes

11. Do we get things done?

    _____ Yes   _____ No   _____ Sometimes

12. Please comment on ways our organization can be improved.

RESOURCES ON THE GIFTED AND TALENTED

Each state has an individual who is responsible for working with gifted and talented programs. For information relating to your state activities, write to your State Department of Education in the state capitol.

American Association for Gifted Children
15 Gramercy Park
New York, NY 10003

Council for Exceptional Children
1920 Association Drive
Reston, VA 22091

National Association for Gifted Children
217 Gregory Drive
Hot Springs, AR 71901

National/State Leadership Training Institute on the Gifted/Talented
c/o Ventura County Superintendent of Schools
County Office Building
Ventura, CA 93001

Office for Gifted and Talented
U. S. Office of Education
400 Maryland Avenue, S.W.
Washington, D. C. 20202

REFERENCES

Gallagher, J. J. *Teaching the gifted child.* Boston: Allyn & Bacon, 1975.

Goldberg, M. L. *Research on the talented.* New York: Bureau of Publications, Teachers College, Columbia University, 1965.

Marland, S. *Education of the gifted and talented* (Report to the Subcommittee on Education, Committee on Labor and Public Welfare, U. S. Senate). Washington, D. C.: 1972.

BIBLIOGRAPHY

T<small>HE</small> <small>FOLLOWING IS</small> an annotated list of selected books and articles that are pertinent to the problems relating to the development of advocacy groups. Other materials are available from national, state, and local advocacy groups.

Advisory groups: New voices gain stature in old power structure. *Nation's Schools*, 1969 *84*, 42.
> Briefly describes the function of the parent-student-faculty advisory board of the Bronx High School of Science of New York and a similar structure, the school-site advisory committee, found in San Francisco high schools. Both organizations handle a wide variety of school problems and issues, ranging from student demands on curriculum to discipline, and appear to have been successful in resolving them.

Alexander, W. M. Community involvement in curriculum. *Educational Leadership*, 1972 29, 655–671.
> Detailing precedents for the then current push for community control of schools, Alexander describes areas in which communities can become involved in the curricula of their schools.

Alinsky, S. D. *Rules for radicals: A practical primer for realistic radicals.* New York: Random House, 1971.
> This book is exactly what it says it is—a practical primer in community organization. Alinksy starts from the way the world is and sets about organizing people to gain power and control over their own lives. He discusses what makes a good organizer, a good organization, a good issue, and the relationship among all three. He analyzes many of the difficult problems such as the age-old ends-means question and communication between individuals with different interests and backgrounds. Throughout the book his vision of the dignity of the individual and the necessity of participation for the renewal of the democratic and creative spirit provides a steady inspiration. More importantly, Mr. Alinsky draws on his experience as the most successful community organizer of his generation to give concrete priorities, perspectives, and tools to future organizers.

Blankenship, A. H. Local school systems benefit by citizenship co-operation. In *Citizen Cooperation for Better Public Schools*, 53rd Yearbook of the National Society for the Study of Education. Chicago: University of Chicago Press, 1954.
> Blankenship's argument is that citizen participation is a vital factor in the proper functioning of local school systems. He calls for advisory roles for citizens and other local groups in matters of curriculum, budget, building, and policy. Perhaps the most important role citizens can play is that of independent, but interested investigators charged with fact-finding and making recommendations. Many case studies of local communities and their citizen committees are cited.

Brinkman, A. R. Cooperative planning strengthens the school program. *National Elementary Principal*, 1957 *36* (1) 167–170.
> The authority role of the professional and the advisory role of the lay community are

emphasized in this article on community councils and joint planning. Brinkman's attitude toward the issue is less oriented toward the necessity and value of community input in decision making than toward the beneficial public relations and support to be gained by school administrators through engaging parents in the making of policy.

Cave, R. G. *Partnership for change: Parents and schools.* London: Ward Lock Educational, 1970.

While this work is concerned with the British school system, many of the situations considered closely parallel American ones. The author is an ardent proponent of parent participation in education. Using the growth of compulsory education in Britain as a framework (a growth he details in the first chapter), Cave, an educator in England, outlines the reasons for increased parental involvement. He discusses how the task of education has become so complex that it can no longer be encompassed by the school alone. He lists and analyzes recent trends in education, including the movement toward citizen participation. He cites concrete examples of what parents have already done to help in the schools and suggests what else they can do. He explains why it is in teachers' best interests to enlist the help of parents and then recommends various ways to involve recalcitrant parents in school activities.

The book is not a complicated, scholarly work; rather it is an operative manual designed for both parents and school officials. Of course the work is most useful to those concerned with citizen participation in Great Britain, but the advice offered seems almost equally applicable to many American communities, if one makes allowance for certain differences, such as racial complications, between the two societies. An added value of the work is the chronological outline it follows, suggesting what both the schools and parents can do at each age to further the development and education of the child. This continues all the way to the career placement for the high school graduate.

Etting, E. E. The board and parent participation. *National Elementary Principal*, 1957, *36* (1)28–30.

The former president of the Board of Education District No. 2 in Scarsdale, New York, makes a strong recommendation for parent input into the activities and decisions of the Board of Education. Etting values parent participation as an asset both to the lay board and to professional educators and teachers. He provides several guidelines for parent involvement, such as defining tasks clearly, diverse membership of lay advisory committees, and involvement of "nonparents" in school groups.

Greenwood, G. E. Some promising approaches to parent involvement. *Theory into Practice*, 1972, *11*, 183–189.

Examines parent involvement at four levels: teacher of the child, volunteer, trained worker, or participant in decision making, especially through advisory board membership. The author, while citing other studies, concentrates on the results of the Follow Through programs of the University of Florida. These programs appear to have had some early success in involving parents in the schools and might serve as a means of comparison for programs adopted elsewhere.

Howe, H., II. Nation of amateurs in education. *School and Society*, 1966, *94*, 448–451.

After commenting on the increasing trend towards specialization and the resultant ever-widening gap between professionals and laymen, the author argues that such a gap is neither beneficial nor justifiable. Among his reasons are a respect for the individual's right to provide for his or her family and a mistrust of professionals. Howe feels that a wide spectrum of individuals can contribute to education in ways that have yet to be tapped.

Howe, H., II. An appeal for agitators. *New York Times,* January 9, 1969, p. 67.
  The former United States Commissioner of Education argues that what education needs most of all is a group of thoughtful and constructive agitators. Howe describes some needs to which agitators might address themselves.

Lurie, E. *How to change the schools.* New York: Random House, 1970.
  A product of Ms. Lurie's 15 years of experience in tangling with "the system," this book is aptly described by its subtitle, "A Parent's Action Handbook on How to Fight the System." She has five children in the New York City public schools, and her emphasis on hard-hitting practical ideas is derived from her conviction that the schools are not good enough for her, or anyone else's, children. Information is included on how the school system functions (and what is wrong with how it functions) in the following areas:

> How to make a school visit
> The curriculum
> Compensatory education and curriculum reform
> Hiring, improving, and firing the staff
> Reporting to parents
> The cumulative record card
> Student suspensions and student rights
> Public hearings
> Parents' rights
> Organizing against the system.

  At the end of each chapter, an "action checklist for parents" is supplied. These lists contain specific suggestions on topics ranging from "what to do if your child is suspended" to "how to prepare for a public hearing."
  Ms. Lurie judges the need for *united* community action to be of paramount importance. Parents are urged to fight for the rights of themselves and their children, beginning with a specific problem that requires attention within their community. While *How to Change the Schools* is particularly valuable for parents in the New York City school system, the tactics suggested would prove helpful to any parent or community group interested in causing change. This is the best available manual for parents interested in school reform.

Organizing the home-school council. *Catholic School Journal,* 1959, *59,* 23–41.
  A manual on how to organize home-school councils to promote understanding between these two entities in the child's life. Written by a guidance group from Marygrove College in Michigan, who apparently have had previous experience in establishing such units, the article has a list of suggestions both for an introductory letter and for the procedure to be followed in the first four meetings.

Pond, M. Z., & Walefield, H. *Citizens survey their school needs.* Columbus, OH: College of Education, The Ohio State University, 1954.
  This monograph, published by the Ohio Center of the Cooperative Program in Educational Administration, seeks to answer concretely questions regarding citizen participation in education: Are citizen advisory councils effective? Can citizens and professionals work together? What concerns should fall under the citizens' jurisdiction and counteract the confusion enveloping this field? To these ends, the Ohio CPEA Center assigned a staff member to work in a community where systematic efforts were made to integrate lay and professional participation in planning school improvement. Part

1 of the monograph is the story of those efforts; it tells how a group of citizens, assisted by the Center's staff member, surveyed their schools and recommended improvements. In Part 2 the citizens' output is analyzed. In all, citizens of three school districts were involved.

The first part of the book is told in the form of an impartial historical narrative, while the second is an empirical analysis. The work is instructive and illuminating and could feasibly serve as a brief manual on citizen participation.

Postman, N. & Weingartner, C. *The soft revolution.* New York: Delacorte Press, 1971.

In the introduction, the authors make it quite clear that *The Soft Revolution* was written for students between 15 and 25 years of age. This is not to imply that no one else can read it, but simply that the ideas and language are directed toward students. The book is a how-to manual for those who are trying to accomplish (or simply are interested in) "the renewal and reconstruction of educational institutions without the use of violence." There is an emphasis on the "judo approach"—a system to induce change without antagonizing those with power and a stake in the status quo. *The Soft Revolution* is a collage of ideas, case studies, philosophy, jokes, rules, and the like and will be of interest to individuals who are attempting to reform the educational institutions through peaceful means.

Thomas, M. P. *Community governance and the school board: A case study.* Austin: University of Texas Press, 1966.

This carefully documented pamphlet is a study of the decision-making role of a school board in Austin, Texas, as related to power blocs within the community. It explores the relationship between school board members and other influential leaders and examines overlapping voluntary associations between school board members and these other leaders on the theory that the network of such associations provides an effective channel for the interchange of opinions. While the discussion is limited to this one community, a number of the findings would seem generally applicable and useful for educational administrators.

INDEX